this Journal Belongs to:

....

....

HI, GOD!

Date ....

Today I...

....
....
....
....

Today I am thankful for...

....
....
....
....

Today I'd Like to pray for...

....
....
....
....

Sketch

AMEN!

HI, GOD!

Date..

Today I...

....

....

....

....

Today I am thankful for...

....

....

....

....

Today I'd Like to pray for...

....

....

....

....

Sketch

AMEN!

HI, GOD!

Date ....

Today I...

....

....

....

....

Today I am thankful for...

....

....

....

....

Today I'd like to pray for...

....

....

....

....

Sketch

AMEN!

HI, GOD!

Date ....

Today I...

....

....

....

....

Today I am thankful for...

....

....

....

....

Today I'd Like to pray for...

....

....

....

....

Sketch

AMEN!

HI, GOD!

Date ....

Today I...

....
....
....
....

Today I am thankful for...

....
....
....
....

Today I'd Like to pray for...

....
....
....
....

Sketch

AMEN!

HI, GOD!

Date ....

Today I...

....
....
....
....

Today I am thankful for...

....
....
....
....

Today I'd Like to pray for...

....
....
....
....

Sketch

AMEN!

HI, GOD!

Date ....

Today I...

....
....
....
....

Today I am thankful for...

....
....
....
....

Today I'd Like to pray for...

....
....
....
....

Sketch

AMEN!

HI, GOD!

Date ....

Today I...

....

....

....

....

Today I am thankful for...

....

....

....

....

Today I'd Like to pray for...

....

....

....

....

Sketch

AMEN!

HI, GOD!

Date ....

Today I...

....
....
....
....

Today I am thankful for...

....
....
....
....

Today I'd Like to pray for...

....
....
....
....

Sketch

AMEN!

HI, GOD!

Date ....

Today I...

....

....

....

....

Today I am thankful for...

....

....

....

....

Today I'd Like to pray for...

....

....

....

....

Sketch

AMEN!

HI, GOD!

Date ....

Today I...

....

....

....

....

Today I am thankful for...

....

....

....

....

Today I'd Like to pray for...

....

....

....

....

Sketch

AMEN!

HI, GOD!

Date ....

Today I...

....
....
....
....

Today I am thankful for...

....
....
....
....

Today I'd Like to pray for...

....
....
....
....

Sketch

AMEN!

HI, GOD!

Date ....

Today I...

....
....
....
....

Today I am thankful for...

....
....
....
....

Today I'd Like to pray for...

....
....
....
....

Sketch

AMEN!

HI, GOD!

Date ....

Today I...

....
....
....
....

Today I am thankful for...

....
....
....
....

Today I'd Like to pray for...

....
....
....
....

Sketch

AMEN!

HI, GOD!

Date ....

Today I...

....

....

....

....

Today I am thankful for...

....

....

....

....

Today I'd Like to pray for...

....

....

....

....

Sketch

AMEN!

HI, GOD!

Date ....

Today I...

....

....

....

....

Today I am thankful for...

....

....

....

....

Today I'd Like to pray for...

....

....

....

....

Sketch

AMEN!

HI, GOD!

Date ....

Today I...

....

....

....

....

Today I am thankful for...

....

....

....

....

Today I'd Like to pray for...

....

....

....

....

Sketch

AMEN!

HI, GOD!

Date ....

Today I...

....
....
....
....

Today I am thankful for...

....
....
....
....

Today I'd Like to pray for...

....
....
....
....

Sketch

AMEN!

HI, GOD!

Date ....

Today I...

....

....

....

....

Today I am thankful for...

....

....

....

....

Today I'd Like to pray for...

....

....

....

....

Sketch

AMEN!

HI, GOD!

Date ....

Today I...

....

....

....

....

Today I am thankful for...

....

....

....

....

Today I'd Like to pray for...

....

....

....

....

Sketch

AMEN!

HI, GOD!

Date ....

Today I...

....
....
....
....

Today I am thankful for...

....
....
....
....

Today I'd Like to pray for...

....
....
....
....

Sketch

AMEN!

HI, GOD!

Date ....

Today I...

....
....
....
....

Today I am thankful for...

....
....
....
....

Today I'd Like to pray for...

....
....
....
....

Sketch

AMEN!

HI, GOD!

Date ....

Today I...

....

....

....

....

Today I am thankful for...

....

....

....

....

Today I'd Like to pray for...

....

....

....

....

Sketch

AMEN!

HI, GOD!

Date ....

Today I...

....

....

....

....

Today I am thankful for...

....

....

....

....

Today I'd Like to pray for...

....

....

....

....

Sketch

AMEN!

HI, GOD!

Date ....

Today I...

....

....

....

....

Today I am thankful for...

....

....

....

....

Today I'd like to pray for...

....

....

....

....

Sketch

AMEN!

HI, GOD!

Date ....

Today I...

....

....

....

....

Today I am thankful for...

....

....

....

....

Today I'd Like to pray for...

....

....

....

....

Sketch

AMEN!

HI, GOD!

Date ....

Today I...

....
....
....
....

Today I am thankful for...

....
....
....
....

Today I'd Like to pray for...

....
....
....
....

Sketch

AMEN!

HI, GOD!

Date ....

Today I...

....
....
....
....

Today I am thankful for...

....
....
....
....

Today I'd Like to pray for...

....
....
....
....

Sketch

AMEN!

HI, GOD!

Date..

Today I...

....

....

....

....

Today I am thankful for...

....

....

....

....

Today I'd Like to pray for...

....

....

....

....

Sketch

AMEN!

HI, GOD!

Date ....

Today I...

....

....

....

....

Today I am thankful for...

....

....

....

....

Today I'd Like to pray for...

....

....

....

....

Sketch

AMEN!

HI, GOD!

Date ....

Today I...

....

....

....

....

Today I am thankful for...

....

....

....

....

Today I'd Like to pray for...

....

....

....

....

Sketch

AMEN!

HI, GOD!

Date ....

Today I...

....
....
....
....

Today I am thankful for...

....
....
....
....

Today I'd like to pray for...

....
....
....
....

Sketch

AMEN!

HI, GOD!

Date ....

Today I...

....
....
....
....

Today I am thankful for...

....
....
....
....

Today I'd Like to pray for...

....
....
....
....

Sketch

AMEN!

HI, GOD!

Date ....

Today I...

....

....

....

....

Today I am thankful for...

....

....

....

....

Today I'd Like to pray for...

....

....

....

....

Sketch

AMEN!

HI, GOD!

Date ....

Today I...

....
....
....
....

Today I am thankful for...

....
....
....
....

Today I'd Like to pray for...

....
....
....
....

Sketch

AMEN!

HI, GOD!

Date ....

Today I...

....
....
....
....

Today I am thankful for...

....
....
....
....

Today I'd Like to pray for...

....
....
....
....

Sketch

AMEN!

HI, GOD!

Date ....

Today I...

....

....

....

....

Today I am thankful for...

....

....

....

....

Today I'd Like to pray for...

....

....

....

....

Sketch

AMEN!

HI, GOD!

Date ....

Today I...

....

....

....

....

Today I am thankful for...

....

....

....

....

Today I'd Like to pray for...

....

....

....

....

Sketch

AMEN!

HI, GOD!

Date ....

Today I...

....
....
....
....

Today I am thankful for...

....
....
....
....

Today I'd Like to pray for...

....
....
....
....

Sketch

AMEN!

HI, GOD!

Date ....

Today I...

....
....
....
....

Today I am thankful for...

....
....
....
....

Today I'd Like to pray for...

....
....
....
....

Sketch

AMEN!

HI, GOD!

Date ....

Today I...

....

....

....

....

Today I am thankful for...

....

....

....

....

Today I'd Like to pray for...

....

....

....

....

Sketch

AMEN!

HI, GOD!

Date ....

Today I...

....
....
....
....

Today I am thankful for...

....
....
....
....

Today I'd Like to pray for...

....
....
....
....

Sketch

AMEN!

HI, GOD!

Date ....

Today I...

....
....
....
....

Today I am thankful for...

....
....
....
....

Today I'd Like to pray for...

....
....
....
....

Sketch

AMEN!

HI, GOD!

Date ....

Today I...

....
....
....
....

Today I am thankful for...

....
....
....
....

Today I'd Like to pray for...

....
....
....
....

Sketch

AMEN!

HI, GOD!

Date ....

Today I...

....
....
....
....

Today I am thankful for...

....
....
....
....

Today I'd Like to pray for...

....
....
....
....

Sketch

AMEN!

HI, GOD!

Date ....

Today I...

....

....

....

....

Today I am thankful for...

....

....

....

....

Today I'd Like to pray for...

....

....

....

....

Sketch

AMEN!

HI, GOD!

Date ....

Today I...

....

....

....

....

Today I am thankful for...

....

....

....

....

Today I'd Like to pray for...

....

....

....

....

Sketch

AMEN!

HI, GOD!

Date ....

Today I...

....
....
....
....

Today I am thankful for...

....
....
....

Today I'd Like to pray for...

....
....
....
....

Sketch

AMEN!

HI, GOD!

Date ....

Today I...

....

....

....

....

Today I am thankful for...

....

....

....

....

Today I'd Like to pray for...

....

....

....

....

Sketch

AMEN!

HI, GOD!

Date ....

Today I...

....

....

....

....

Today I am thankful for...

....

....

....

....

Today I'd Like to pray for...

....

....

....

....

Sketch

AMEN!

HI, GOD!

Date ....

Today I...

....

....

....

....

Today I am thankful for...

....

....

....

....

Today I'd Like to pray for...

....

....

....

....

Sketch

AMEN!

HI, GOD!

Date ....

Today I...

....
....
....
....

Today I am thankful for...

....
....
....
....

Today I'd Like to pray for...

....
....
....
....

Sketch

AMEN!

HI, GOD!

Date ....

Today I...

....

....

....

....

Today I am thankful for...

....

....

....

....

Today I'd Like to pray for...

....

....

....

....

Sketch

AMEN!

HI, GOD!

Date ....

Today I...

....

....

....

....

Today I am thankful for...

....

....

....

....

Today I'd Like to pray for...

....

....

....

....

Sketch

AMEN!

HI, GOD!

Date ....

Today I...

....

....

....

....

Today I am thankful for...

....

....

....

....

Today I'd Like to pray for...

....

....

....

....

Sketch

AMEN!

HI, GOD!

Date ....

Today I...

....

....

....

....

Today I am thankful for...

....

....

....

....

Today I'd Like to pray for...

....

....

....

....

Sketch

AMEN!

HI, GOD!

Date ....

Today I...

....
....
....
....

Today I am thankful for...

....
....
....
....

Today I'd Like to pray for...

....
....
....
....

Sketch

AMEN!

HI, GOD!

Date ....

Today I...

....

....

....

....

Today I am thankful for...

....

....

....

....

Today I'd like to pray for...

....

....

....

....

Sketch

AMEN!

HI, GOD!

Date ....

Today I...

....
....
....
....

Today I am thankful for...

....
....
....
....

Today I'd Like to pray for...

....
....
....
....

Sketch

AMEN!

HI, GOD!

Date ....

Today I...

....

....

....

....

Today I am thankful for...

....

....

....

....

Today I'd Like to pray for...

....

....

....

....

Sketch

AMEN!

HI, GOD!

Date ....

Today I...

....
....
....
....

Today I am thankful for...

....
....
....
....

Today I'd Like to pray for...

....
....
....
....

Sketch

AMEN!

HI, GOD!

Date ....

Today I...

....
....
....
....

Today I am thankful for...

....
....
....
....

Today I'd Like to pray for...

....
....
....
....

Sketch

AMEN!

HI, GOD!

Date ....

Today I...

....

....

....

....

Today I am thankful for...

....

....

....

....

Today I'd Like to pray for...

....

....

....

....

Sketch

AMEN!

HI, GOD!

Date ....

Today I...

....
....
....
....

Today I am thankful for...

....
....
....
....

Today I'd Like to pray for...

....
....
....
....

Sketch

AMEN!

HI, GOD!

Date...

Today I...

....
....
....
....

Today I am thankful for...

....
....
....
....

Today I'd Like to pray for...

....
....
....
....

Sketch

AMEN!

HI, GOD!

Date ....

Today I...

....

....

....

....

Today I am thankful for...

....

....

....

....

Today I'd Like to pray for...

....

....

....

....

Sketch

AMEN!

HI, GOD!

Date ....

Today I...

....
....
....
....

Today I am thankful for...

....
....
....
....

Today I'd Like to pray for...

....
....
....
....

Sketch

AMEN!

HI, GOD!

Date ....

Today I...

....
....
....
....

Today I am thankful for...

....
....
....
....

Today I'd Like to pray for...

....
....
....
....

Sketch

AMEN!

HI, GOD!

Date ....

Today I...

....

....

....

....

Today I am thankful for...

....

....

....

....

Today I'd Like to pray for...

....

....

....

....

Sketch

AMEN!

HI, GOD!

Date ....

Today I...

....
....
....
....

Today I am thankful for...

....
....
....
....

Today I'd Like to pray for...

....
....
....
....

Sketch

AMEN!

HI, GOD!

Date ....

Today I...

....

....

....

....

Today I am thankful for...

....

....

....

....

Today I'd Like to pray for...

....

....

....

....

Sketch

AMEN!

HI, GOD!

Date ....

Today I...

....

....

....

....

Today I am thankful for...

....

....

....

....

Today I'd Like to pray for...

....

....

....

....

Sketch

AMEN!

HI, GOD!

Date ....

Today I...

....
....
....
....

Today I am thankful for...

....
....
....
....

Today I'd like to pray for...

....
....
....
....

Sketch

AMEN!

HI, GOD!

Date ....

Today I...

....

....

....

....

Today I am thankful for...

....

....

....

....

Today I'd Like to pray for...

....

....

....

....

Sketch

AMEN!

HI, GOD!

Date ....

Today I...

....

....

....

....

Today I am thankful for...

....

....

....

....

Today I'd Like to pray for...

....

....

....

....

Sketch

AMEN!

HI, GOD!

Date ....

Today I...

....
....
....
....

Today I am thankful for...

....
....
....
....

Today I'd Like to pray for...

....
....
....
....

Sketch

AMEN!

HI, GOD!

Date ....

Today I...

....

....

....

....

Today I am thankful for...

....

....

....

....

Today I'd Like to pray for...

....

....

....

....

Sketch

AMEN!

HI, GOD!

Date ....

Today I...

....
....
....
....

Today I am thankful for...

....
....
....
....

Today I'd Like to pray for...

....
....
....
....

Sketch

AMEN!

HI, GOD!

Date ....

Today I...

....
....
....
....

Today I am thankful for...

....
....
....
....

Today I'd Like to pray for...

....
....
....
....

Sketch

AMEN!

HI, GOD!

Date ....

Today I...

....
....
....
....

Today I am thankful for...

....
....
....
....

Today I'd like to pray for...

....
....
....
....

Sketch

AMEN!

HI, GOD!

Date...

Today I...

....
....
....
....

Today I am thankful for...

....
....
....
....

Today I'd Like to pray for...

....
....
....
....

Sketch

AMEN!

HI, GOD!

Date ....

Today I...

....

....

....

....

Today I am thankful for...

....

....

....

....

Today I'd Like to pray for...

....

....

....

....

Sketch

AMEN!

HI, GOD!

Date ....

Today I...

....
....
....
....

Today I am thankful for...

....
....
....
....

Today I'd Like to pray for...

....
....
....
....

Sketch

AMEN!

HI, GOD!

Date ....

Today I...

....

....

....

....

Today I am thankful for...

....

....

....

....

Today I'd Like to pray for...

....

....

....

....

Sketch

AMEN!

HI, GOD!

Date ....

Today I...

....

....

....

....

Today I am thankful for...

....

....

....

....

Today I'd Like to pray for...

....

....

....

....

Sketch

AMEN!

HI, GOD!

Date ....

Today I...

....
....
....
....

Today I am thankful for...

....
....
....
....

Today I'd Like to pray for...

....
....
....
....

Sketch

AMEN!

HI, GOD!

Date ....

Today I...

....

....

....

....

Today I am thankful for...

....

....

....

....

Today I'd Like to pray for...

....

....

....

....

Sketch

AMEN!

HI, GOD!

Date ....

Today I...

....

....

....

....

Today I am thankful for...

....

....

....

....

Today I'd Like to pray for...

....

....

....

....

Sketch

AMEN!

HI, GOD!

Date ....

Today I...

....
....
....
....

Today I am thankful for...

....
....
....
....

Today I'd Like to pray for...

....
....
....
....

Sketch

AMEN!

HI, GOD!

Date ....

Today I...

....

....

....

....

Today I am thankful for...

....

....

....

....

Today I'd like to pray for...

....

....

....

....

Sketch

AMEN!

HI, GOD!

Date ....

Today I...

....
....
....
....

Today I am thankful for...

....
....
....
....

Today I'd Like to pray for...

....
....
....
....

Sketch

AMEN!

HI, GOD!

Date ....

Today I...

....
....
....
....

Today I am thankful for...

....
....
....
....

Today I'd Like to pray for...

....
....
....
....

Sketch

AMEN!

HI, GOD!

Date ....

Today I...

....

....

....

....

Today I am thankful for...

....

....

....

....

Today I'd Like to pray for...

....

....

....

....

Sketch

AMEN!

HI, GOD!

Date ....

Today I...

....

....

....

....

Today I am thankful for...

....

....

....

....

Today I'd Like to pray for...

....

....

....

....

Sketch

AMEN!

HI, GOD!

Date ....

Today I...

....
....
....
....

Today I am thankful for...

....
....
....
....

Today I'd Like to pray for...

....
....
....
....

Sketch

AMEN!

HI, GOD!

Date ....

Today I...

....

....

....

....

Today I am thankful for...

....

....

....

....

Today I'd Like to pray for...

....

....

....

....

Sketch

AMEN!

HI, GOD!

Date ....

Today I...

....
....
....
....

Today I am thankful for...

....
....
....
....

Today I'd Like to pray for...

....
....
....
....

Sketch

AMEN!

HI, GOD!

Date ....

Today I...

....

....

....

....

Today I am thankful for...

....

....

....

....

Today I'd Like to pray for...

....

....

....

....

Sketch

AMEN!

HI, GOD!

Date ....

Today I...

....

....

....

....

Today I am thankful for...

....

....

....

....

Today I'd Like to pray for...

....

....

....

....

Sketch

AMEN!

Made in the USA
Las Vegas, NV
18 April 2022